How to find Business Partners on Internet

Top 139 E-Commerce and B2B Marketplaces

Tamara Vuorinen

Contents

Disclaimer

The author/publisher takes no responsibility for the content or correctness of any websites mentioned in "How to find Business Partners on Internet".

Under no circumstances shall the author be held liable for any consequence of visit/use websites/services mentioned in the book.

Notice on Internet resources

This book contains lots of links and all these links to resources on Internet are checked by author. But Internet resources changes all the time. Please let me know if some of links are not correct. Email address: info@newexportmarket.com

Preface

You can find all of the information that you need to conduct global business on the Internet. But, the Internet, like the Universe, is huge! There are thousands of B2B websites and it would be time consuming to go through every one of these sites. This book contains tips about the biggest B2B Marketplaces, E-Commerce websites, Online Shopping Malls, B2B Directories, Business Networks, B2B Websites, Online Fairs, Business Communities and Business Databases around the globe. I do not strive to present all B2B Marketplaces and directories worldwide, as this is an impossible task. I decided to write this book after 6 years of blogging on the subject. The B2B Marketplaces and other websites that I describe in this book are the result of my extensive research on the Internet.

Author

The author lives in Stockholm, Sweden. She graduated from Stockholm International Business School as an Export Manager. The author became inspired by the huge success of online dating sites for individuals and founded the B2B website www.newexportmarket.com for businesses. Since 2010, she has been blogging about B2B Marketplaces, E-Commerce sites and Business Matchmaking online. Now, the first book about B2B Marketplaces and finding business partners online is published.

Target Group

This book is targeted to small and medium sized businesses, entre-preneurs, business minded individuals, export managers, purchasing managers, exporters, importers, traders, sellers and buyers. Thus, the book is dedicated to everyone who has passion for global business.

Why you should read this book

You will learn how to find business partners online. After reading this book, you wouldn't need to hire an expensive export consultant, because you will be able to do this work yourself. This book will teach you about the biggest B2B Marketplaces, E-Commerce sites, Business Directories and B2B websites across the globe. You will also learn helpful tips for running background checks on companies and avoid being cheated.

Chapter 1. What's a B2B Marketplace and E-commerce?

Some Business is just meant to be.

A simple definition of B2B Marketplace - a website where suppliers and buyers meet each other and conduct business.

E-Commerce – a website that enable companies and individuals to conduct business. E-Commerce operates in all marketing segments: B2B, B2B2C, B2C, C2C and C2B.

There are so many solo entrepreneurs and businesses that need partners around the globe. Do you want more business and to make more money? Of course – that's what all companies want. But, how do you find a trustworthy partner that you can do business with?

That's where B2B Marketplaces and E-Commerce websites come into the picture. What are you waiting for? Create a profile on one of the B2B Marketplaces below and become visible for business owners worldwide. Describe your ideal partner and be sure to include your most important keywords, products, services and markets in your company profile. Choose your words carefully – because all the words you use in your profile will be searchable by others members of this B2B website.

B2B Marketplaces offer the following services and products: Memberships, Business Directories (Search in directory by continent, country, region, product, product category, industry, keyword), contact to other members, Virtual Meetings/Live Chat, Forum, Verified Suppliers, Ordering Credit Reports, Email Alerts, Advertising, Own Website, Showrooms, Product Catalog, Listings, Buy and Sell leads, Own online store/shops, Payment services, Guidelines for safety trade. Some B2B marketplaces and E-Commerce websites offer also logistics solutions.

What kind companies register on these B2B Marketplaces? All kind businesses: manufacturers, service providers, traders, exporters, importers, retailers, wholesalers, distributors, agents and buying offices.

You will find all these B2B Marketplaces and E-Commerce websites listed below and organized by Alexa rank and continent or countries.

Chapter 2. Top B2B Marketplaces and E-Commerce websites in US and Canada

Never miss a chance to do business.

www.amazon.com + various national websites. Alexa rank 6 (2016). E-Commerce, B2B2C Marketplace, launched 1995. Amazon is world's largest online retailer and has lots of product lines, stores, subsidiaries in different countries. Amazon offers great solutions for sellers. Start selling on Amazon is easy and you will reach millions of Amazon customers. Selling on Amazon is a four-step process after registering you as Seller: List your products – Sell – Ship- Get Paid. Amazon can also do shipping for you or arrange it yourself. Alternatively build your Amazon Web store – online e-commerce platform for your business. Learn more on Amazon website- choose "Make Money with us" and then" Sell on Amazon".

www.eBay.com Alexa rank 24 (2016). E-Commerce, Online Auction. Launched 1995. One of world's largest marketplaces for both individuals as well businesses. More than 650 million items are listed on eBay. Over 145 million active international buyers are doing business on the website. Services: Auction, Product Listings, eBay Store and much more. In eBay store you can display all items you will sell and that will maximize your business on eBay. Please read more about Bidding, Buying, Selling, creating an eBay store, fees on eBay/Help.

www.etsy.com Alexa rank 143 (2016).Global Marketplace for unique items. Launched 2005. Etsy is focused on handmade and vintage items, also unique factory-manufactured items under Etsy's guidelines. Vintage items have to be at least 20 years old. You can buy and sell art, photography, clothing, jewelry, food, crafts, bath and beauty products, quilts, knick-knacks and toys. Sellers allowed to create own shop, but listings of products cost. Learn more about selling on Etsy – please read Sellers Handbook on the website. Etsy is a certified B Corporation — a new kind of company that uses the power of business to solve social and environmental problems.

www.overstock.com Alexa rank 602 (2016). Online shopping. Overstock is also known as its shortcut O.co. Launched in 1999. Over 1 million products are registered on the site. Overstock offers international shipping to over 100 countries through partnership with e-commerce provider Border Free. Check out World stock (Fair trade) – there artisans around the globe are selling handmade products. Overstock is more than online store- find Pet Adoptions and Farmers Market (artisanal food) on the site.

www.manta.com Alexa rank 2213 (2016). Business Directory. Manta is large online community for small business in US. Looking for businesses in US – Manta is the best place to start searching. Browse 22 million US companies. Type the product/service and location in Search and you will get huge number of results. Manta offers following services: Company Profile, Member Profile, Business Listings and Manta Connect. Follow and participate in interesting conversations with other business owners in Manta Connect – online community on the website. Manta Worldwide – browse companies in Canada, United Kingdom and in Australia.

www.globalsources.com Alexa rank 6025 (2016). Globalsources was founded in 1971 and website launched in 1999. B2B Marketplace. Looking for suppliers in China and Asia? Join Buyer Community on Global Sources and find reliable suppliers. Other services: Publisher of print and digital magazines, sourcing reports, organizer of sourcing fairs, private sourcing events, trade shows. For more information please view video" *Importers Guide to Global Sources Services" on Corporate info – Products on the website. More than 250000 suppliers and 1 million international buyers are registered on the website.* Global Sources has 60 offices worldwide. Global Sources is publicly listed on the NASDAQ since 2000.

www.hoovers.com Alexa rank 8464 (2016). Business Database and Directory. Launched 1990. Subsidiary of Dun & Bradstreet. Hoovers is a business research company that provides insight and information about industries, companies and decision makers. Want to build a list of prospects? Use Lead Builder and create your list in minutes. Hoovers offers following services: credit reports, company information, lead lists. There are 85 million corporations across 900 different industries in Hoovers' database. Every businessman should read Hoovers Business Blog - Bizmology – The Science of business intelligence. Valuable reading for everyone who is doing business.

www.business.com Alexa rank 12580 (2016). Marketplace for business purchases. Browse in business directory to find products, compare prices and make your buying decision. Over 30 million buyers from small-to-medium visit the website to purchase the products they need to run and grow their businesses. Business.com drives more than half a million purchases a year, generating over $1.5 billion in sales for 10,000+ advertisers.

www.salespider.com Alexa rank 13239 (2016). Based in Canada. Sales Spider - business social network for Small and Medium Sized Businesses (SMBs) with over 1,400,353 members. Services: Chat Forums, Business Library, Business Directory (over 37 million companies), Free Classified Marketplace (B2B Advertising), Leads Directory and much more.

www.americanapparel.net Alexa rank 13857 (2016). American Apparel is an American clothing manufacturer, distributor and retailer – an industrial revolution. Made in US - production is in US. The company is vertically integrated – it takes care of everything: manufacturing, design, marketing, accounting, retail and distribution. See the wholesale catalog and check out their upcoming trade shows. American Apparel distributes its products to wholesale customers worldwide. The company has global offices in Canada, Mexico, Japan, UK and Switzerland. A sales office and distribution center with showroom in Düsseldorf serves European customers. Find your nearest store in Store Locator.

www.thomasnet.com Alexa rank 15888 (2016). Product sourcing and Supplier discovery platform. Before known as "Thomas register of American manufacturers", first published in 1898 by Harvey Thomas. Online from the mid of 1990. Thomasnet is designed for procurement professionals and engineers. Lots of valuable services, tools and resources: CAD Register, Free Profiles, Guides, Advertising, Product Showcase Solution and much more. Over 700000 industrial and commercial suppliers are registered on the website. 1800000 industrial buyers are visiting Thomasnet every month. You can download Cad drawings from different manufacturers; choose your own among millions of 2D, 3D Models.

www.ariba.com Alexa rank 16402 (2016). Ariba – cloud-based business commerce network. The platform supports both sellers and buyers. Sellers can manage catalogues, bids, purchases, invoicing and buyers can search for suppliers, negotiate savings, procure goods and services and track spend.

www.ecrater.com Alexa rank 20438 (2016). Online shopping mall and marketplace. Founded 2004 by Dimitar Slavov. eCrater is an e-commerce website builder - get your own online store on eCrater. Great solution for sellers who don't have a standalone retail website. eCrater has launched marketplaces also in Australia and UK. Use the feature - eBay importer and you can easily import the products from your eBay store into eCrater.

www.businessseek.biz Alexa rank 26592 (2016). Small Business Directory & Search Engine. Over 34400 businesses in 1338 categories registered. Services: advertising, listings, article/press release submission, website submission, homepage text links.

www.liquidation.com Alexa rank 29916 (2016). A Liquidity services and online auction marketplace where buyers can source inventory for resale on other marketplaces. More than 1 million registered buyers. Liquidation.com offers following bulk wholesale merchandise: surplus inventory, refurbished, returns, closeouts, salvage, new and used products in many different categories. Most of auctions started at 100 USD and the final price will decided by bidding buyers on the marketplace. New auction have been added daily to marketplace. If you wish international shipping – please check the phrase "Available for Export" in shipping detail section in every auction. Check also if you can ship merchandise to your country. See the Table country list (Liquidation. com doesn't ship to these countries). Sellers of this merchandise are retailers, manufacturers, public sector agencies, logistics providers, service companies and financial institutions.

www.efactor.com   Alexa rank 32041 (2016). Entrepreneurial community. Mission of Efactor is to inspire, connect and support entrepreneurs. Be inspired: read blogs, see videos on the website and visit events. Get deals – find helpful products regarding funding, pitching, business planning, ideation, start business etc. Connect with right people for you - other entrepreneurs, investors and mentors.

www.importers.com   Alexa rank 69287 (2016). B2B Marketplace and Import Export Directory, online since 1995. Are you a seller? Find G20 importers on this B2B website. Importers is a global trade platform for small and medium sized enterprises with focus on G20 economies. Lots of useful info on Trade Resources: B2B leads, trade news, international trade links, country specific information, trade development organizations (international and national), commodity prices, transportation and customs.

www.leadferret.com   Alexa rank 71753 (2016). Founded 2011. Free B2B Database. Contains 15 million records with company, name, title, address, phone number and most importantly email address. View tutorial videos on Leadferret Youtube page. LeadFerret has partnered with SalesNexus, web-based CRM and email marketing company. See other interesting partners such as SalesScripter, RapidBuyR, Precise-Hire, Experian and SalesDog on the LeadFerret website.

www.buyerzone.com   Alexa rank 79542 (2016). Buyerzone is a premier B2B lead generation company that provides leads to over 8500 businesses. This B2B marketplace makes it easy to buy for buyers- they get free price quotes from competing vendors. Sellers get verified quality leads. Find high-quality trade partners on the website. Download free reports and quick guides about B2B lead generation; see infographics and view webinars on Buyerzone website. Find useful info in Buyerzone's lead generation blog.

www.tradeford.com   Alexa rank 92540 (2016). B2B Marketplace. Trade and manufacturer Directory. TradeFord provides global importers with information on products, exporters, suppliers. You can use following resources on Tradeford: B2B Directory, Chamber of Commerce Directory, Freight Forwarders Directory, Seaports Directory and Trade Show Directory, different Lead generation programs: Quote Connect, Quote Connect Express, Email Connect, Content Connect and Data Connect.

www.toptenwholesale.com   Alexa rank 105693 (2016). Sourcing Platform and Wholesale Website. Toptenwholesale connects re-sellers with manufacturers, wholesalers and importers with suppliers. The company is based in Los Angeles and also has offices in China, India, Colombia, Mexico, Bangladesh, Philippines and Vietnam. Toptenwholesale offers lots of services: Supplier Pass® verified membership for suppliers;   Shipping, Warehousing and Logistics; Custom Sourcing; Trade Show organizing for international companies.

Choose verified supplier when you are doing business. Supplier Pass® Premium Members are Suppliers that have passed a Company Profile Verification (CPV) by an accredited third-party agency. The authenticity of supplier's corporate information is verified before the Supplier Pass® verification is issued.

www.manufacturer.com Alexa rank 166043 (2016). Global Trade Platform that connects buyers with verified suppliers around the globe. Are you looking for products produced in US – you can find these using service Made in USA. If you are a seller you should try the Premium membership and you will receive more contacts with buyers. Premium Membership offers lots of benefits as unlimited listings and upload of videos. Only Premium members can apply for Supplier Pass®. Suppliers with Supplier Pass® have passed an authentication & verification process. Buyers can identify these suppliers by the Supplier Pass® icon displayed in their listings. Manufacturer offers lots of different services: logistics, shipping, warehousing, matchmaking events, buyer introductions, factory introductions and much more. Manufacturer is owned by JP Communications Inc. JP Communications also launched TopTenWholesale in 2005.

www.globalbx.com Alexa rank 236308 (2016). Free business for sale listing exchange that connects business sellers with business buyers, brokers and lenders. Sell your business online. Lots of useful information for sellers and buyers of business. See Buyers' Guide, Sellers Guide and Franchise guide on the site. Globalbx can also help you with commercial loans and financing.

www.biznik.com   Alexa rank 276570 (2016). Entrepreneurial community. Created by married couple Lara Feltin and Dan McComb in 2005. Biznik is a community of indie business people – solopreneurs, freelancers, independent contractors and companies-of-one. Memberships are Basic, Pro and ProVip. Visit Biznik events, participate in discussions in BizTalk – Community Forum and publish business articles on Biznik website. Biznik is a great resource for all indie businesses.

www.toboc.com   Alexa rank 430531 (2016). Headquarter in Montreal, Canada and branch office in Bangalore, India. Service for sellers: Showcase unlimited products and send trade enquires. Customer support team will match products posted by sellers with available buy offers. Service for buyers: post your buy requirements and get response from lots of verified suppliers.

www.worldbid.com   Alexa rank 430969 (2016.) B2B and B2G Marketplace in Canada. Worldbid offers lots of free services and features for exporters, importers and traders: trade leads, showrooms, product directories and country directories.

www.fuzing.com   Alexa rank 783985 (2016). B2B Marketplace where buyers and suppliers come together to meet in a "virtual tradeshow". Read how to succeed as a supplier and buyer on Fuzing. It's easy to create an extended profile and it's free. Create also "Alerts" and you will be notified by email when suppliers or buyers post listing in your category or industry.

Chapter 3. Top B2B Marketplaces and E-commerce websites in China

Never give up. Today is hard, tomorrow will be worse, but the day after tomorrow will be sunshine. (Jack Ma, Founder of Alibaba Group).

www.aliexpress.com Alexa rank 51 (2016) - Global consumer marketplace where consumers can by products at wholesale prices directly from manufacturers and wholesalers. Part of Alibaba group. Find super deals daily up to 50-70% off on this marketplace. Online Shopping for cheap automotive, phones, accessories, computers, electronics, fashion, beauty, health, home, garden, toys, sports and other merchandise.

www.alibaba.com Alexa rank 62 (2016). #1 B2B Marketplace and e-commerce giant. Named after poor woodcutter Ali Baba from folk tale "Ali Baba and the forty thieves". He discovered the secret of thieves – phrase" Open Sesam" and found a treasure. Alibaba has 90 offices in mainland China and 19 offices outside mainland China. Headquarter is situated in Hangzhou. Millions of products in 40+ categories are for sale on this global trade platform. International buyers from 190+ countries are visiting this marketplace daily. Alibaba is a part of Alibaba Group that was founded by former English teacher Jack Ma and other 18 people in 1999. The vision is "To make it easy to do business anywhere". Alibaba Group employed over 22000 people around the world and operates following various businesses: Taobao. com - Online shopping for Chinese consumers; Tmall.com - Premium Shopping for Chinese consumers; Juhuasuan.com - Flash sales and group buying site; 1688.com - Online wholesale marketplace in China; Alimama.com -Online marketing technology platform that offers marketing services for sellers on Alibaba marketplaces; Aliyun.com - Developer of platforms for cloud computing; Alipay.com – provider secure payment services for Alibaba Group marketplaces; Cainiao.com – Operator of logistics information platform which provides real time access to information for sellers, buyers and traders.

Over 40 million global buyers access marketplaces free. As seller you can choose different kind memberships on Alibaba: Unverified member, Verified member or Gold Supplier. As a buyer you can apply for AliPrimeBuyer membership and get personalized service, exclusive networking opportunities tailored sourcing events and much more. AliPrimeBuyer members are verified by Alibaba. Alibaba offers also inspection service for buyers. You can order this service directly on Alibaba from 3rd party inspectors. These inspectors can visit manufacturers, ports anywhere in China to make reports including photos of ordered goods.

www.dhgate.com Alexa Rank 1330 (2016). Wholesale Marketplace which is headquartered in Beijing. Founded in 2004 by Diane Wang, current CEO and Asia's most powerful business woman. DHgate claims to have about 25 million product listings from over 900000 Chinese suppliers and 4 million buyers from 230 different countries based on figures from 2011 (Wikipedia). One of world's leading B2B online trading marketplaces for goods made in China. Buy high quality China wholesale apparel, cell phones, electronics, handbags, wedding dresses and other products directly from Chinese manufacturers. Free shipping and payment protection. Membership in DHgate VIP Club offers services to most frequent buyers. Each time you buying on DHgate, you are awarded a DHgate score.

The more you trade, the more you benefit. Read more about this program for buyers on DHgate. DHgate is using Escrow system that protects buyer's transaction. How it works? Buyer place an order – buyer pays DHgate – seller ships the order – Dhgate holds payment until buyer approves order. In 2011 DHgate was recommended by the Chinese Ministry of Commerce as one of China's Top 4 E-Commerce Platforms for International Trade.

www.made-in-china.com Alexa rank 2117 (2016). B2B Marketplace that connects worldwide buyers with Chinese manufacturers, suppliers, sellers and traders. Launched in 1998 and headquartered in Nanjing. Over 3 million suppliers are listed in Product Directory on the site. Services for buyers:

• Bonus Points – earn virtual points.

• Trading services: Product sourcing, Background reports of supplier.

• Secure payment service Escrow: Made-in-china will release payment to the supplier after buyer's confirmation of the product quality and shipment.

Services for suppliers:

• Auditing service by 3rd party inspection company SGS (auditing firm based in Switzerland). Be SGS audited supplier.

www.diytrade.com Alexa rank 7560 (2016). Global B2B Trading platform and largest China product directory. It was launched in 1999 as eBigChina.com and renamed to Diytrade.com in 2006. Diytrade has over 1,5 million members from more than 200 countries.

Diytrade offers following memberships: Free Member – you can build your own website on Diytrade.com with free sub-domain and Biz Member - you can post more products and enjoy priority listing right.

Value added services:

• DIY-shop, your online store, free to use for Biz members.

• Third Party Biz Verify –gain buyers confidence by having identity and legitimacy verified.

• Hot Product promotion – showcase the product in Hot Product section.

Read more about value added services on Diytrade website.

www.hktdc.com   Alexa rank 8705 (2016). B2B Marketplace with head office in Hong Kong. Sourcing from 120000+ quality suppliers in Hong Kong. HKTDC is short name for Hong Kong Trade Development Council, established in 1966. It has more than 44 offices around the world whereof 13 on the Chinese mainland. HKTDC promotes Hong Kong as a platform for doing business with Asia and China. Enter Small Order Zone to see what product you can order in small quantities on the marketplace. See Hot Deals – some items with price 1 USD are for sale, free shipping. HKTDC organizes lots of trade shows, events, conferences every year in Hong Kong and also overseas.

HKTDC services:

• E-Magazines –view these online, in your mobile or read printed copies. Free subscription.

• Buyer meetings – sourcing experts arrange face-to-face meetings between buyers and suitable suppliers.

• Business matching - business matchmaking team identifies suitable suppliers in Hong Kong.

• Buyer rewards program – a privilege program for professional buyers. Source on HKTDC and earn points. See fabulous rewards options on the website. Earn gifts by sourcing.

www.taiwantrade.com.tw   Alexa rank 20619 (2016). Official trade portal of Taiwan, founded 2002. Taiwantrade has 60 worldwide offices. Services for buyer members: Free membership; Search suppliers and products and Post buying leads.

Search assistance - fill in an online form regarding your request/product and Taiwantrade will revert to you with proposals.

Biz Exchange – an online bulletin board to post trade leads and view offers.

E-books – download these and view Taiwan products online.

Click on www.idealez.com , B2B shopping website and find premium Taiwanese suppliers. IdealEZ is implemented by Taiwantrade.

www.toocle.com Alexa rank 43901 (2016). B2B Directory and Search Engine. Toocle – a trading circle of global suppliers around one buyer. Toocle is a provider of platform for business communication between global buyers and suppliers. Services for buyers: create your own Toocle of suppliers, post request, publish procurement information, compare prices and contact suppliers. Services for sellers: join buyers Toocle, create your product catalog, receive buyer inquiry and chat live with buyers.

www.globalmarket.com Alexa rank 27528 (2016). M2B Marketplace (Manufacturer to Business). Founded in 2002 and located in Guangzhou. All manufacturers have been audited by TUV Rheinland, leading certification company and got GMC certificate. GMC is shorted Global Manufacturer Certificate. GlobalMarket also brings out GMC mall – M2C (Manufacturer to Customer) on M2cmart.com. At the moment GMC mall specializes on kitchen, textile, furniture, batch, appliance and lamps. All products from GMC manufacturer are tested throw quality control system. GlobalMarket merged with TradeEasy.com in 2008.

www.hisupplier.com Alexa rank 53118 (2016). B2B Marketplace and China suppliers' directory. Products and Services for Sellers:

You can design company website with your own domain name using site design function on HiSupplier. Free site – free membership with extension service of ten optimized products.

Premium service – Gold site, Platinum site, Diamond site, optimization of keywords and Google sitemap.

Value added services – Top site; will be on the first page of searching results. See more services under pricing structure. Services for Buyers: Post a buying leads, Browse Chinese products in the Product directory (26 product categories) and create Trade alerts of products you are interested in.

www.ecvv.com Alexa rank 74350 (2016). B2B Marketplace. Established in 2003. 2,5 million registered users according to numbers from 2011. Ecvv offers lots of different services for buyers and suppliers. I should like to describe more their BV verification process for suppliers. Ecvv cooperates with BV- Bureau Veritas which is a leading verification organization in the world. BV will perform verification process as independent 3rd party and after that submit verification. BV-verified suppliers have higher credibility and they get an icon which distinguishes them from other not verified suppliers. Do you want better rank for your product listings and get more clicks from buyers? Ecvv offers Hot rank premium service. See the service fees for different ranking on the site. Do you want to export to China? Ecvv can help you to start export to Chinese market with following services: Face-to-face meeting and Promotion seminar arrangements, China office establishment and much more. Premium seller services: China Premium supplier, Credit pass, Export to China and Business services. Memberships for Premium China suppliers: Gold, Platinum and Diamond.

Buyer Basic services: Searching products, manufacturers by keyword in Product directory or Hot catalog. Sending inquiries and posting buyer lead. Face-to-face meetings between buyers and suppliers arranged by Ecvv. Premium Buyer services: Purchase assistance, Translation and various Business services.

www.tradett.com Alexa rank 103308 (2016). B2B Marketplace, China manufacturer's directory and China products directory. Online trading platform between Global buyers and China manufacturers, exporters, suppliers, traders.

Services for Buyers: search products in the directory, contact suppliers, post trade leads, offer to buy in Offer Board, get support through

Trade resources.

Services for Suppliers: add products to Product directory (China suppliers) and to Trade offers directory (Global suppliers); search Global buyers in Trade offers directory.

www.etradeasia.com   Alexa rank 66002 (2016). B2B Marketplace, Taiwan. Launched 1997 and owned by Asiannet Inc. EtradeAsia has over 1 million members and about 1,8 million products listed on the website. Gold membership for suppliers – top ranking on the website. Advertising on website and on search listing page – product pictures, banners.

www.busytrade.com Alexa rank 165959 (2016). B2B Marketplace and Manufacturer directory where you can buy China wholesale products from Chinese wholesalers. BusyTrade has over 3 million registered users of which 320000 + are outside mainland China. BusyTrade has also launched 7 websites in other countries: China, Hong Kong, Japan, India, Bangladesh, Mexico and Brazil. Do you want to be agent for BusyTrade in your country? Read more about agent program on BusyTrade website. Busytrade offers following memberships: Platinum, Gold, and Silver for China Suppliers and China pass; Global Pass for Global suppliers. Suppliers can also apply for certification by 3rd party certification company to get certified supplier icon.

Following services are offered for Global Buyers: Company DIY website, Premium buyer, Buyer-Seller matching conference and Translation service.

Busytrade has BusyDollar system on its platform. BusyDollars is virtual money that can be used on Busytrade marketplace, read more about this on the website.

Sourcing services according to an ASP model. GlobalMarket also merged with B2S.com in 2008. B2S is a trade portal connecting buyers with suppliers in 5 industries: Lighting, Home Electrical, Components, Electronics and Gifts & Home.

Chapter 4. Top B2B Marketplaces and E-Commerce websites in India

Make business happen.

www.indiamart.com   Alexa rank 965 (2016). B2B Marketplace. Launched in 1996 by Dinesh Agarwal. Indian largest online marketplace with over 1,5 million registered suppliers. Company has over 2600 employees in 40 offices in India. Solutions and services for sellers:

- Online catalog – publish 400 products to your catalog, company profile, zoom up for product view. TrustSEAL for Suppliers – Third party verified TrustSEAL report.

- Maximizer – get maximum benefits and value.

- Star Supplier – get higher listing and more business.

- Leading Supplier– Showcase as industry leader and get premium listing.

For buyers:

- Submit your Buy Requirement. If you can't find suitable supplier, contact Buyers Helpdesk. Over 5 million buyers have made purchases on Indiamart.

Indiamart launched in 2014 a new B2B E-Commerce site www.tolexo.com . India's online store for Business and Industry.

www.tradeindia.com   Alexa rank 3325 (2016). B2B Marketplace, launched in 1996 by Bikki Khosla.

Products and services:

- Online Catalog - this is a virtual showroom with company profile, product description and photos.

- Exporters Yellow Pages - contains info about 2 million Indian Exporters.

- Exim CD-ROM – contains information about Indian sellers and buyers, foreign sellers and buyers. Database is updated quarterly.

- Directories of manufacturers, suppliers and business services.

- Tradeindia rewards – earn points on every activity.

Find distributors on www.getdistributors.com which is an initiative by Tradeindia. Do you looking for distributors, sales agents or franchisees? Or you will be a distributor/ sales agent – then you should visit this website.

Premium Memberships – Platinum and Gold, read more on the website.

Services for Buyers: Post your Buy Requirement; Call DialB2B (get suppliers info via SMS/email); Buyers Helpdesk; Subscribe to Trade Alerts (get sell offers). Search in Comprehensive and Updated Indian Manufacturers Directory. Search in Online Catalogs. Order Credit Reports.

Services for Sellers: Super Seller (lots of benefits); Premium Seller; Trust Stamp (verification); Online Catalog; Post your products; Search buyers in database; advertise on Tradeindia; Post Freight Quotes and Subscribe to trade Alerts (get relevant buy offers).

www.exportersindia.com Alexa rank 11602 (2016). B2BMarketplace, launched 1997. Search for Manufacturers, Suppliers, Exporter, Importers, and Service Providers in Indian Business directory and Foreign Business directory.

ExportersIndia offers 3 memberships: Silver, Gold and Platinum with following services:

• Templates based website – get your website.

• Banner advertisements – build brand awareness.

• Live chat – integrates to your mobile phone or GTalk (Gmail).

• Vtrust certificate – Verified suppliers are buyers first choice.

• Flip book – ExportersIndia designs an interactive brochure about your business that can be used online/offline.

• Google 360 degree – takes your customers on a virtual tour to your business.

• Responsive website – the website that perfectly fits in different screen sizes as smartphone, tablet.

www.bizbilla.com Alexa rank 25826 (2016). B2B online marketplace where business from around the world can trade and gain information on global businesses. Bizbilla also offers Business tools that can help business owners create websites, convert currency and provide government related information. Bizbilla is a free B2B marketplace to use, just simply sign up for access to various products and service.

www.go4worldbusiness.com Alexa rank 56132 (2016). B2B Marketplace. One of 114 trade portals which are owned by Wyzen Systems Pvt.Ltd. Founded in 1997 and based in New Delhi.

Network of 114 Regional and Country Trade portals around the globe. See more info on the website.

Over 552000 companies from 240 countries and over 285000 products are registered on the site.

Memberships: Gold, Silver and Free. Services:

Company profile displayed on all 114 Trade Portals in network.

Contact members and chat with members.

Your company presentation and much more. Click on New pricing on the website.

www.infobanc.com   Alexa rank 66007 (2016). Founded 1997 and owned by Ace InfoBnc Ptd.,   a Business information company.

Infobanc offers following Business information, Services and Tools:

- Information - Business Opportunities, Tenders (Institutional Procurement information), Latest Export Import Data, Market information and much more.

- B2B Directories of All Buyers, Overseas Importers, Indian Buyers, Buyers by category, buying agents, and Distributors.

- Trade leads by country, region, Indian states and category.

Wholesale B2B Marketplace www.bazara2z.com is also promoted by Ace InfoBnc Ptd. Other websites launched by Ace InfoBnc: Ficci-b2b.com (Business organization) and Vanik.com (Agents, Distributors).

Infobanc website contains lots of useful information for Exporters and Importers.

www.indiabizsource.com Alexa rank 73310 (2016).B2B Marketplace and B2B Directory for Manufacturers, Suppliers, Wholesalers and Exporters. Owned by Integrated Databases India Ltd and India Today Group, based in New Delhi.

Services for Buyers: Search by company or product name; contacts suppliers with "Send Enquiry" button; browse by Suppliers and Sell Offers.

Services for Sellers – different Website packages, Premium listings, Email marketing, SEO, Banner and Mobile solutions.

Chapter 5. Top B2B Marketplaces and E-commerce websites in Asia (excl. China and India)

Amazing B2B World.

www.rakuten.com Alexa rank 1607 (2016).B2B2C Marketplace (Online Shopping in US). Founded in 1997 and owned by Rakuten Inc., based in Japan. The Japanese word "rakuten" means optimism. Definition of B2B2C is Business to Business to Consumer. This is a business model: a business which has a product partner with other business, for example e-commerce platform to sell this product to consumers.

In 2010 Buy.com joined Rakuten family and one of the world's largest marketplaces was born. Rakuten offers more than 90 million products to consumers from over 38500 merchants around the globe. Rakuten ranks among top 3 online shopping sites in the world. Currently Rakuten supports over 5500 shop owners on the marketplace.

Services for retailers:

•   Retailers can create own online shops on the Rakuten platform.

•   Marketing Tools – BuyMail (emailmarketing); Storefront (fully branded and image focused); Shipping Engine (create own shipping rules) and ECCs, ecommerce consultants – they are there to help merchants.

P.S. Merchants need to have a US bank account; US tax ID and US shipping location.

Services for shoppers:

•   Rakuten Super Points – earn Super Points by shopping and use these like cash later.

If you want to buy from Japan, please visit Rakuten Global Market www.global.rakuten.com

www.ecplaza.net Alexa rank 8766 (2016). Wholesale B2B Marketplace and Trade Mall. Marketplace was launched in 1996, Trade Mall in 2004. Based in South Korea. Over 1 million members from 230 countries are registered on the website. Ecplaza is connected to network of 50 global agents. Ecplaza offers Free, Silver and Gold memberships with lots of benefits for its users. Other services: EDI, trade consulting and lots of offline services.

For Buyers – use Trade Mall, marketplace for one stop sourcing at wholesale prices. No charge for Buyers. Pay simply through PayPal. Buy high quality Korean products.

For Sellers - sell your products on Trade Mall. Use the delivery service you want. You will get paid through PayPal so you need to have or create an account on PayPal.

www.tradekorea.com Alexa rank 12106 (2016). International E-trade Marketplace, owned by KITA, Koreas International Trade Association, based in South Korea. Services:

- KITA E-pay solution - online credit card payment solution.

- Global Business Matching - free service for Buyers.

- Credit Points – earn credits and use these to purchase of services.

Membership: Trader, Gold Trader and Gold Pus Trader.

www.ec21.com Alexa rank 25929 (2016). B2B Marketplace. Launched in 1997 and based in South Korea. Over 2,5 million Buyers and Sellers from 245 countries are registered on the website. EC21 offers Free, TradeOK and TradePro memberships. Services:

- Credit report – Different types of reports: Biz- Check, Quick-Rate and Fullcheck.

- TradeVerify - Authentication and Verification service of businesses. Your company will highlighted with TradeVerify mark on EC21.

- Korea market Research.

- World Trade Zone (WTZ) – online and offline catalog magazine. View the catalog online in E-book showroom.

www.gobizkorea.com Alexa rank 26478 (2016). International Trade website runs by Small and Medium Business Corporation, government agency of South Korea. Buyers will found over 60000 Korean products on this website. Services:

- BMS Business Matchmaking Service – free service for foreign buyers run by Korean Government Agency (Small and medium Business Corporation).

- VAP Visitor assistance program – free service for foreign buyers visiting Korea, funded by Korea Government Agency.

- Video Meeting – free E-trade video meeting solution. Connect with Korean suppliers with help of English Korean interpreter on-line. All you need for video meeting is PC, Webcam and headset.

- Exhibition – lots of services as Online Exhibitions, Online Product gallery, Promotion Videos, Trade shows in your country and Korea Youth Enterprise Gallery.

www.lazada.com Alexa rank 31923 (2016). Online Shopping Mall based in Malaysia. Launched by Lazada Group in 2012. Lazada is growing rapidly and has over 2000 employees. No.1 Shopping mall in South East Asia countries: Malaysia, Singapore, Vietnam, Philippines, Indonesia and Thailand. Only domestic shipments in above-mentioned countries. Unfortunately international shipments are not available on Lazada. This shopping mall offers lots of products that are suitable as corporate gifts at best prices for businesses.

www.buykorea.org Alexa Rank 55752 (2016). B2B Marketplace, operated by Kotra, Korea Trade Investment Promotion Agency, based in South Korea. Over 100000 Korean companies are looking for global Buyers on this website. Kotra has a large overseas network in 84 countries.

This marketplace offer following services for users:

• EMS Delivery – if seller uses EMS delivery buyer can truck your shipments online.

• KOPS Kotra online payment service – order payment with your credit card.

www.kmall24.com Alexa rank 85894 (2016). Online Shopping Mall. Founded in 2014 and owned by Korea International Trade Association. Based in South Korea.

Why choose this Online Shopping Mall? Kmall24 offers following services:

• Best Korean producers at best price.

• Unique Korean products only available on Kmall24.

• Customer service in buyer's location – Kmall24 has lots of marketing offices around the world.

- Comfortable shopping experience for shoppers.

- Convenient mobile access everywhere – buyers can access Kmall24 also from smart devices.

www.arbet.am   Alexa Rank 596743 (2016). Armenian Business Directory. Launched in 2006 by company Ventus Systems LLC. Based in Armenia which is located in South Trans-Caucasus. Totally over 3200 companies are registered on this website. Database of Armenian manufacturers, exporters, importers and service providers.

Chapter 6. Top B2B Marketplaces and E-Commerce websites in Latin America

Success is often achieved by those who don't know that failure is inevitable. (Coco Chanel).

www.mercantil.com Alexa rank 61116 (2016). Business Portal based in Chile. The largest database of Chilean companies. Mercantil offers following products: Corporate video, Virtual catalogs and Banner advertising.

www.mercatrade.com Alexa rank 497259 (2016). B2B Marketplace. Founded in 2009 by Emmanuel Beserve and Patricia Maroday in Panama. Meet Importers and Exporters in Latin America. More than 22000 companies are registered on this marketplace. Mercatade offers following membership plans: Free, Premium Pro and Premium Platinum.

Services and tools:

- Publication of your product in the "Featured products" or "Featured Suppliers" section.

- Product API (Web application) – install API and import thousands of your products or whole Product catalog from your website to Mercatrade marketplace in seconds.

- User friendly company showroom.

- Verified members – get a Mercatrade Verified seal.

- Credit Reports - made by third party agency Global Authentication A&V.

- Premium customer support.

- Advertising – different advertising packages.

www.brazilbiz.com.br Alexa rank 999285 (2016). B2B Marketplace, Brazil. Do you want to enter Brazilian market? Get a free quotation for Brazilian trade consulting services on the website.

www.venexport.com   Alexa rank 1534560 (2016). B2B Directory, Venezuela. Venezuelan Industry and Business opportunities Directory. Easy to navigate and find Venezuelan companies on this site.

Chapter 7. Top B2B Marketplaces and E-Commerce websites in Africa

Business is more exciting than any game. (Lord Beaverbrook).

www.africa-business.com   Alexa rank 268416 (2016). African Business Pages, founded in 1995. Business Directories of all African countries. If you are looking for agents and distributors in Africa –you should visit this website. Services and features:

- Download business directories of African countries in Excel format.

- Business Guide Africa - read online; advertise your products in this Guide and reach 15 countries in Africa. Featured listings and companies. Advertise your products for free.

www.matchdeck.com   Alexa rank 418650 (2016). Business Matching Platform. This B2B Matching engine connects you to other companies according to your business objectives. Matchdeck uses data analytics and algorithms to match and connect businesses to each other. In 2015 Matchdeck acquired aiHit - the world's largest business search engine with over 16 million companies worldwide.

www.bestsaexporters.com   Alexa rank 619844 (2016). Manufacturer Directory. Looking for import from South Africa? Find a lots of export-ready manufacturers on this website.

www.southafricab2b.co.za   Alexa rank 809166 (2016). B2B Portal, South Africa. This Marketplace is part of International B2B Network Tradeholding.com. More than 620900 companies are registered on this website. Browse in directory by continent, country, trade leads, biz keywords, top products and top searches. Features and benefits:

- Credit based charging system – earn credits and use these to post trade leads and respond to other members.

- Credit Packages – order additional credits.

- Free website and Product catalog.

- Premium listings – list your products and leads on the top of similar ads.

- Bidding feature – higher rank of your product/lead in your category and search results.

Memberships: Top member (Silver, Gold and Platinum).

Chapter 8. Top B2B Marketplaces and E-Commerce websites in Middle East

Business opportunities are like buses, there's always another one is coming. (Richard Branson).

www.egypt-business.com Alexa rank 66740 (2016). Business Directory. Based in Cairo, Egypt. Operates by Marketing Börse Gmbh. Looking for business partners in Egypt? Visit this online directory of Egyptian companies. Find also tenders, events and other valuable info about Egypt on this B2B website.

www.tradekey.com Alexa rank 102482 (2016). B2B Marketplace. Launched in 2006 in Saudi Arabia. One of world's fastest growing B2B portal with 7,7 million users around the world.

Memberships:

- Goldkey plus - lots of valuable features: product website, video, brochures, unlimited access to buyers and much more.

- Goldkey – online product showroom, connect live with buyers, get a DRM – Dedicated Relationship Manager for support.

- Silverkey – access over 3 million buyers from 240 countries, get a virtual trade office.

- TKDigitals – Digital marketing services.

Services and features:

- TradeMate – Trade Messenger (beta version). Download your TradeMate for free and chat with your potential business partners.

- Community – TradeKey has lots of different forums on its website such as Trade, Industry, Regional and Safe Trading forums. Do you have questions about trading? Ask Trade experts and get valuable tips in Trade forum.

- Learning center – guide how to use TradeKey platform, learning videos.

www.qataronlinedirectory.com Alexa rank 114310 (2016). Business Directory. Based in Qatar. Online database and guide to business in Qatar. Learn more about Qatar – you will find lots of useful information about this country on this site.

www.tradeturkey.com Alexa rank 440091 (2016). B2B Marketplace. TradeTurkey.com is one of 114 global trade portals which are operated by Wyzen Systems Pvt.Ltd., India. Find Turkish buyers, suppliers, products and also global trade leads on this platform.

www.iraqdirectory.com Alexa rank 634184 (2016). Business Directory. Iraqdirectory.com is your guide to Iraq business. Business directories of Iraq companies and international suppliers. Find also Iraq business news on this website.

www.tradeegypt.com Alexa rank 645547 (2016).B2B Directory. Based in Egypt. Are you a global buyer and looking for Egyptian suppliers? You should visit this online database of Egyptian exporters.

Chapter 9. Top B2B Marketplaces and E-Commerce websites in Europe

Passion for business.

http://een.ec.europa.eu   Alexa rank 835 (2016). Enterprise Europe Network (EEN). Launched in 2008 and based in Grenoble, France. Largest information, consultancy and innovation support network in Europe. EEN has six hundred Member Organizations across EU and beyond where over 4000 business advisors are working. Mission of EEN – help small companies to develop their business.

Services:

- Going International – Business matchmaking services: Business database and matchmaking events. Find a local EEN contact point in your country.

- Technology transfer – EEN can help you with technology, innovation or business application for your business.

- Access to finance – evaluation of your company's financial situation, finding venture capital and public financial aid.

- Research funding – participating in EU- funded research projects.

- EU law and standards – Information about laws, regulations in EU.

- Intellectual property rights (IPR) – help with commercializing of new idea, service and product. Protecting your intellectual property.

- Events Calendar - find events in EU.

- Business database – search among thousands of company profiles.

www.dawanda.com   Alexa rank 2691 (2016). Marketplace for hand-made products. Based in Germany but also offices in France, Spain and Poland. There are 3,8 million registered members and more than 240000 shops on the marketplace. You can sell or buy on Dawanda following products: unique products – not mass produced, handmade, refurbished, products designed by you and vintage (at least 20 years old). Services and Tools for sellers:

- Own shop on Dawanda – open your shop just in minutes. Personalize it with shop banner. List your products.

- Wirecard – enable wirecard in your shop and offer more payment methods for your customers.

- Dawanda app – with this app you can show off your Dawanda shop on your own Facebook Page.

- Dawanda Widget – using this widget you can share your shop on your own website or blog.

- Payment with Smartphone – accept credit card or EC payments on your Smartphone or tablet.

www.kompass.com   Alexa Rank 4652 (2016). B2B Portal. Based in France but the website is available in 26 different languages. Kompass has over 60 years' experience in providing global business information. This global B2B Database' company has a unique classification system – SIC codes and covers more than 60 countries. Kompass contains over 4 million company profiles in 65 different countries around the globe – see Global Coverage on this website. Subscriptions:

- Basic – Web presence.

- Premium – Web communication.

Solutions:

- TOP 3 – appear in TOP 3 companies in search results or other activity.

- TOP link – promotion in top link section.

- Video broadcast in Kompass network.

- Advertising – promote your company in this global B2B database.

- Lead generation and marketing – run campaigns on the website.

- Direct marketing – use millions of email addresses on the site.

- Web analytics.

www.esources.co.uk Alexa rank 58069 (2016). Wholesale Directory. Based in United Kingdom. Business Directory of verified wholesale suppliers, drop shippers, wholesale offers and trade leads. Buyers can source wholesale merchandise, stock lots and clearance lines on ESources.

Products and services:

- Memberships – Basic Buyer and Premium Buyer membership, Basic Supplier and Premium Supplier membership.

- TradePass™ - verification of supplier.

- Auction Houses Directory – find auctioneers and Auction Houses in UK. See upcoming auctions and Auction venues.

www.europages.com Alexa rank 97854 (2016). B2B Trade Platform. Over 30 years' experience and based in France. International Database that contains approximately 2,6 million companies mainly from European countries. Tools for content creation and multilingual search engine in 26 different languages. One of the largest B2B websites in the world that helps small businesses to be found on the European market. Europages has partner network in more than 20 countries. Services:

- Get found – be visible for 33 million visitors /year. Europages attracts so many visitors and has 122 million page views/year.

- Showcase your products with a catalog – let the Europages build a professional catalog for you.

- Advertising – banners.

- Reach customers with emailing.

www.businessmagnet.co.uk Alexa rank 110543 (2016). B2B Directory. United Kingdom. Over 140000 members have registered and listed their products/services in over 75000 categories on this website. Businessmagnet has a huge amount data on its website so the directory is segregated into 5 specific indexes. These are Search index, Company index, Product index, Town index and Postcode index. So you are able to browse by Company, Product, Town and Postcode using these indexes.

Memberships: Free, Basic, Advanced and Premium.

www.tradeboss.com Alexa rank 131290 (2016). Global B2B Marketplace. Launched in 2002. Part of Tradeholding.com network. Based in Romania. Browse worldwide by continent, region, country, product, industry and keyword on Tradeboss site.

Services: Fee website, free product catalog. Top member -Silver, Gold and Platinum memberships.

www.imexbb.com   Alexa rank 161632 (2016). B2B Marketplace. Launched 1996 and based in Switzerland. Import Export Bulletin Board is a free service for international buyers, sellers and investors. Imeexbb connects also entrepreneurs and investors around the globe. Find new business opportunities by browsing leads on this website.

www.zentrada.eu   Alexa rank 186155 (2016). Wholesale Marketplace and European Trading network. Based in Germany. Zentrada is a leading Buyer network for wholesale purchase of consumer goods for retailers in Europe. Zentrada has offices in 7 countries: Germany, Netherlands, Spain, Italy, France, Poland and Hungary. Zentrada connects small retailers with large suppliers throughout Europe. More than 300000 commercial retailers use this marketplace for their purchases.

www.tradeholding.com Alexa rank 201579 (2016). International B2B Network. Based in Romania. Tradeholding has lots of regional portals such as Europe.bloombiz.com, ulfbusiness.tradeholding.com (Middle East), wtpfed.tradeholding.com (Greece & Turkey) and much more.

www.approvedbusiness.co.uk Alexa rank 217346 (2016). B2B Directory. Founded 1992 in United Kingdom. Business Directory contains over 55000 companies in UK. Over 30000 products and services in 30 industry sectors are listed on this website. Services:

• Listings – Free, Standard and Featured.

• Banner advertising.

• Free Press Release on the website.

• Review of companies – submit your review of other company you had relation to.

www.achilles.com Alexa rank 248596 (2016). Global Business Network of industry communities, based in UK. Achilles employs 950 people in 22 countries and offers global procurement services with local expertise.

www.rusmarket.com Alexa rank 310406 (2016). B2B Marketplace. Launched 1998 in Russia. Find business partners in Russia, Baltic, CIS European countries, Kazakhstan and also worldwide on this marketplace.

www.wholesalepages.co.uk Alexa Rank 353207 (2016). Wholesale Suppliers Directory and Wholesale Network in United Kingdom.

You can find here UK suppliers, exporters, drop shippers, wholesalers, importers, distributors, manufacturers, and overstock, surplus and clearance sources.

Browse by company, product, brand, category, location or Trade Leads in this online directory. Find also international drop shippers in France, USA and Hong Kong. Are you interested in Auction Houses? See the UK Auction directory and the International Auction directory on the site. Wholesale pages has also UK Car Boot Sales Directory.

Memberships for Buyers: Bronze, Silver, Gold and Lifetime.

Memberships for Sellers: Free Seller and Premium Seller.

There is lots of useful information in Wholesale Learning Centre on this website.

www.golden-trade.com Alexa rank 400276 (2016). Marketplace for French speaking countries. Based in France. Totally 11 sales offices in following French speaking countries : France, Belgium, Switzerland, Canada, Morocco, Algeria, Senegal, Burkina Faso, Republic Democratic of Congo, Ivory Coast, Mali, Caribbean and Reunion Island & Indian Ocean. Network of 1700 agents in 40 countries.

Memberships: Free, Premium and Customized Services. Looking for an agent in French speaking countries? Products of registered members will be seen by Golden-Trade's agents in 40 different countries on this website.

www.baltic-leads.com   Alexa rank 759713 (2016). Baltic Business Portal. Find business partners in Baltic Countries – Estonia, Latvia and Lithuania. Get useful business information about this region.

Chapter 10. B2B Marketplaces and E-Commerce websites in Australia and New Zealand

Winners never quit and quitters never win. (Vince Lombardi).

www.industrysearch.com.au   Alexa rank 219717 (2016). Industrial B2B Directory. Hub of industrial sourcing and Australian's leading industrial B2B website. Launched in 1998. Over 1 million members have registered on this website. Discover 50000 listed products and services. Browse in Australian Supplier Directory and find business partners in transport, mining, construction, manufacturing, engineering, farming and other industry sectors. You can also buy used machinery and equipment here.

www.australiatradenow.com   Alexa rank 458419 (2016). B2B Portal. One of 114 portals operated by Wizen Systems Pvt.lts., India. Find Australian buyers, suppliers, product and trade leads on this B2B Marketplace.

www.hospitalityhub.com.au Alexa rank 588305 (2016). Hospitality B2B Directory based in Australia. Over 2000 registered suppliers and 5000 listed products.

www.medicalsearch.com.au   Alexa rank 599494 (2016). Medical B2B Directory of Australia. Hub of medical sourcing with 3000 registered suppliers. Over 10000 medical products/services are listed on this B2B website.

www.nzdirectory.co.nz   Alexa rank 832046 (2016). B2B Directory, New Zealand. NzDirectory is a local directory that contains over 400000 New Zealand's businesses. This website showcasing the New Zealand's products and services to the world.

Chapter 11. Industry B2B Marketplaces, Wholesalers and Trade Shows

Success is walking from failure to failure with no loss of enthusiasm. (Winston Churchill).

www.cebit.de Alexa rank 33805 (2016). CeBit – Global event for digital business. The world's largest computer expo in Hanover, Germany.

www.fibre2fashion.com Alexa 39398 (2016). B2B Marketplace for garment, textile and fashion, India. Over 1800 products are listed in 13 categories.

www.asdonline.com Alexa rank 117640 (2016). ASD - the leading retail merchandise trade show for consumer goods in Las Vegas, US.

www.clothing-dropship.com Alexa rank 277904 (2016). Global clothing mall, fashion wholesaler, China. Operates by Wd.cm – an online fashion clothing wholesaler company.

Services:

• Dropshipping – high quality products from factory with lots of stocks, upload to eBay or Amazon directly.

• Lots of different payment methods.

• Shipments to your county – see more info on the website.

www.ironplanet.com Alexa rank 61070 (2016). IronPlanet – B2B online auction solution for buyers and sellers of used heavy equipment in US and Ireland, Europe. Looking for trucks, tractors, trailers, excavators or other heavy equipment? Visit Ironplanet's online auctions and bid directly from your computer.

www.nuorder.com Alexa rank 123071(2016). B2B E-commerce platform based in US. Fashion wholesale marketplace for retailers and brands. Request a free demo to get started. Support team can also personally guide you throw set up process. Nuorder provides live training lessons for customers. Features and tools:

- Order management - view, edit, copy, cancel, export your orders.

- Reporting tools - real time reports, report builder.

- Easy to use product catalog.

- Create line sheets.

www.rockanddirt.com Alexa rank 124721 (2016). Rockanddirt – used and new heavy construction equipment marketplace based in US and Canada. Caterpillar, Bobcat, loaders, cranes, barges, forklifts, sawmills, elevators, trucks, trailers and heavy equipment parts – all this equipment you can sell, buy or lease on Rockandirt.

www.magiconline.com Alexa rank 173572 (2016). Magic is the world's largest fashion marketplace, comprised of eleven unique communities showcasing the latest in apparel, footwear, accessories, and manufacturing in US.

www.mfg.com Alexa rank 231170 (2016). MFG is a manufacturing marketplace that brings manufacturing and procurement professionals together. The B2B marketplace is the right place for all manufacturing needs. Offices in US, China and France.

MFG is a B2B marketplace with some integrated features that makes buying and selling a little easier. Some of these tools include:

Easy click quoting system; Quote tracking feature; Buyer and supplier ratings; RFQ Creation to receive quotes for custom parts and Integrated part library.

www.mesteel.com Alexa rank 267925 (2016). Mesteel – steel online marketplace in Middle East. Dubai, UAE.

www.italianmoda.com Alexa rank 379599 (2016). B2B Fashion Marketplace. This marketplace is for wholesale buyers who are searching "Made in Italy" fashion and textiles. Find factories, suppliers, brands of Italian fashion, clothing, textiles, bags, shoes, jewelry, accessories and lingerie. Italianmoda has network of 10 marketplaces for example Vigevanoshoes.com; USStyle.com and SpanishModa.com – see more network websites on the marketplace.

www.offpriceshow.com Alexa rank 908202 (2016). Off price show for retailers offering goods for 20-70% below wholesale cost. This is a marketplace number one for fashion wholesale.

Chapter 12. How to find Trade Shows, Fairs and other Business Events

If you cannot do great things, do small things in a great way. (Napoleon Hill).

Are you looking for trade shows, fairs, exhibitions, conferences, networking meetings, global seminars, workshops, business matchmaking events or other B2B events? You can search these business events by country, industry or venues on websites below. Are you an organizer of business events? Add your event to these websites and get more visitors and exhibitors to your event.

www.10times.com Alexa rank 10738 (2016). 10times is one of the largest business event discovery platform. Based in India.

www.eventseye.com Alexa rank 32403 (2016). Eventseye is a Trade Show Directory and its ambition is to cover major Trade Exhibitions all over the planet.

www.tsnn.com Alexa rank 196054 (2016). Tsnn is a global up to date tradeshow database and member of the Tarsus Group Plc with offices in US, UK, France, Germany, UAE and China.

www.businessglobal.com Alexa rank 201683 (2016). Businessglobal is an online exhibition provider. Businessglobal hosts permanent country and industry online exhibitions all year round for 24 hrs a day and 7 days a week.

www.tradeshowalerts.com Alexa rank 337210 (2016). Based in Delhi, India. Tradeshow alerts is one of the largest Tradeshow directory online.

www.bvents.com Alexa rank 746780 (2016). Bvents is a free world-wide source for events and trade shows. Search for trade shows or add your event.

Chapter 13. Organizers of Exhibitions, Forums, Events and Trade Fairs

A person who never made a mistake never tried anything new. (Albert Einstein).

www.reedexpo.com   Alexa rank 197896 (2016). Reed Exhibitions - organizer of exhibitions with a portfolio of 500 events in 41 countries and a staff over 3000 exhibition specialists. For example National Hardware Show in Las Vegas is organized by Reed Exhibitions.

www.centrallia.com Alexa rank 4015344 (2016). Centrallia, based in Canada is an organizer of global B2B forums that generate new business opportunities for companies.

www.futurallia.com Alexa rank 7259817 (2016). Futurallia, based in France - organizer of International B2B networking events that offers one-on-one meetings. More than 45 forums has been organized in different countries since 2003.

Chapter 14. How to find Investors and co-founders for your start up

Introduce your start-up to the world!

www.killerstartups.com Alexa rank 47756 (2016). Killerstartups is an online publication and community for Internet entrepreneurs. Submit your start-up and get it discovered by investors and potential customers. Killerstartups is a part of a family of sites including Fundable.com, Launchrock.com and Bizplan.com.

www.crowdcube.com Alexa rank 55608 (2016). Crowdcube is one of the world's leading investment crowdfunding platform. The company enables anyone to invest alongside professional investors in start-up, early stage or growth businesses through equity, debt and investment fund options.

www.founder2be.com Alexa rank 185066 (2016). Founder2Be – the fastest way to found the co-founders for your start-up. Meet over 50000 co-founders on this platform. Based in Helsinki, Finland. One of the largest start-up community for developers, web designers, marketers and anyone looking to start a start-up worldwide.

www.mycapital.com Alexa rank 375427 (2016). Mycapital - Venture Capital Network for raising venture capital. Send email to over 3000 venture capitalists. Search in Directory of venture capital firms and angel investors.

www.angelinvestmentnetwork.us Alexa rank 1081163 (2016). Angel Investment Network helps entrepreneurs and investors to build profitable relationships. Find angel investors globally or locally – submit your proposal and connect to over 11500 investors.

www.companypartners.com Alexa rank 1252742 (2016). Find business angels, partners or mentors for your start-up or growing business on Companypartners.

www.businesspartners.com Alexa rank 2122090 (2016). Businesspartners is a global community for entrepreneurs to find investors and partners.

Chapter 15. How to protect against Fraud

Don't be victim of fraud or scams.

www.experian.com Alexa rank 5340 (2016). Experian - leading global information services' company, providing data and analytical tools to clients around the world. Experian helps businesses and consumers to manage credit and prevent fraud.

www.dnb.com Alexa rank 25504 (2016). D&B (Dun& Bradstreet Corporation) is the world's leading source of commercial information and insight on businesses. Think about this - every day 260 businesses fail to bankruptcy. D&B products:

- D-U-N-S® Number - this unique nine-digit identification number for businesses worldwide.   Worldwide network™ – an alliance of commercial information providers covering more than 190 countries.

- DUNSRight® - process that transforms business information. Global Database – source of local and global business, contains more than 225 million business records.

- Lots of different solutions: Business Credit Report; Sales &Marketing; Supply Management; Fraud, Waste and Abuse Prevention etc. Before your start a new business get your credit report in minutes.

www.wymoo.com   Alexa rank 2510238 (2016). Wymoo conducts background checks and comprehensive investigations in over 100 countries.

Chapter 16. Business Networks, Search Engines, Magazines and other useful sources for Exporters and Importers

Opportunities don't happen. You create them. (Chris Grosser).

www.yellowpages.com Alexa rank 977 (2016). Yellow pages (YP.com) – Business Directories Worldwide.

www.entrepreneur.com Alexa Rank 1231 (2016). Website was launched in 1997 and YoungEntrpreneur.com launched 1999. This magazine is a premier resource for small businesses. "Top 50" - read about amazing entrepreneur stories that got most page views. "How to" – there are lots of invaluable tips for every entrepreneur. Advertise on Entrepreneur Magazine, visit events and meet other entrepreneurs. Entrepreneur magazine has international editions in China, Middle East, Mexico, Philippines and South Africa. Want to know what brands are most trusted – please see the "Lists" on the website.

www.yandex.com Alexa rank 1873 (2016). Russian Search Engine. Yandex also operates in Ukraine, Kazakhstan, Belarus and Turkey.

www.shopping.com Alexa rank 13364 (2016). Price comparison site, part of eBay Commerce Network. This site allows the customers shop online for the best deals and lowest prices.

www.bni.com Alexa rank 139462 (2016). BNI – Business Network International – referral organization with over 185000 members in 60 countries. BNI's philosophy is "Givers Gain"- members are giving referrals to other members to build relationships and receive referrals in return.

The organization works by creating a group of people (chapter) from various industries and encouraging regular passing of referrals.

www.worldstopexports.com Alexa rank 195263 (2016). World's top exports (WTex) publishes latest statistics and research about international business. Read articles on this site or request your own research.

www.new.ewomennetwork.com Alexa rank 275439 (2016). Ewomennetwork – women's business network in North America. The network helping members to acquire more customers, market their businesses and access to resources.

www.worldbusinessculture.com Alexa rank 591409 (2016). Worldbusinessculture contains information on business culture in 39 different countries.

Chapter 17. Glossary

You don't have to know everything. You just have to know where to find it. (Albert Einstein).

Alexa traffic rank - a rough estimate of website's popularity.

B2B – Business to Business - commercial transactions between businesses.

B2B Leads – see buying lead and selling lead definition below.

B2B2C - Business to Business to Consumer.

B2B Marketplace – platform for commercial transactions between businesses.

B2C – Business to Consumer – transactions between businesses and consumers. Businesses selling to consumers.

B2G – Business to government –Businesses selling products and services to government.

Bizmology – a business blog (Dun & Bradstreet) about business intelligence on Hoovers.com.

Buying lead – purchase request of product/service published by buyer.

Bureau Veritas – offers testing, inspection and certification services.

Business Database – organized collection of data of businesses.

Business Directory - listing of businesses by category.

Business Listing – list businesses within some category.

Car Boot sales – individuals selling household and gardening goods from car's boot.

C2B – transactions between consumer and business.

C2C – transactions between consumers.

Classified advertising – advertising which may be distributed free of charge.

Clearance sales – a sale of goods at reduced prices to get rid of superfluous stock or because the shop is closing down.

Company Profile – presentation of company.

Crowdfunding - the practice of funding a project or venture by raising monetary contributions from a large number of people, today often performed via Internet-mediated registries, but the concept can also be executed through mail-order subscriptions, benefit events, and other methods. Crowdfunding is a form of alternative finance, which has emerged outside of the traditional financial system. (Wikipedia).

Drop shipping - direct delivery of goods from the manufacturer to the retailer or customer.

E-Commerce - commercial transactions conducted electronically on the Internet.

Flash sales –"Deal-of-the-day is an E-commerce business model in which a website offers a single product for sale for a period of 24 to 36 hours. Potential customers register as members of the deal-a-day websites and receive online offers and invitations by email or social networks". (Wikipedia).

Group buying – "also known as collective buying, offers products and services at significantly reduced prices on the condition that a minimum number of buyers would make the purchase". (Wikipedia).

M2B - Manufacturer to Business – Manufacturer selling to businesses.

M2C – Manufacturer to Customer.

Member Profile – presentation of registered company/member at B2B Marketplace.

Online catalog – a list of company's products or services online (often with pictures).

Overstock - a stock that is larger than demand.

SGS – inspection, verification, certification and testing company.

Selling Leads - provided by Seller including info about Minimum Order Quantity (MOQ), Delivery Lead-time and payment method.

Surplus – a quantity excess of what is required.

Trade leads – indication or suggestion about potential business.

Chapter 18. Table of B2B Marketplaces, E-Commerce Websites, B2B Directories, Business Networks, Communities and Online Shopping Malls with Alexa Global rank

Alexa traffic rank is a rough estimate of this site's popularity.

The rank is calculated using a combination of average daily visitors to this site and page views on this site over the past 3 months. The site with the highest combination of visitors and page views is ranked #1. See more on www.alexa.com

Alexa traffic rank is changing all the time. When you are reading this book the Alexa rank for these sites can be different. If you want to know actual Alexa traffic rank please visit Alexa.com.

Period: from 2016

Website/Company	Alexa rank	
Amazon	6	B2B2C
eBay	24	B2B2C, Auction
Aliexpress	51	Wholesale Platform
Alibaba	62	B2B Marketplace, E-commerce
Etsy	143	Handmade and Vintage Marketplace
Overstock	602	Online shopping
Entrepreneur	755	Magazine
Enterprise Europe	835	Consultancy Network
Indiamart	965	B2B Marketplace

Yellow Pages	971	Business Directory
Dhgate	1330	Wholesale Marketplace
Rakuten	1606	B2B2C E-commerce platform
Made-in-China	2117	B2B Platform
Manta	2213	Business Directory
Dawanda	2691	Marketplace for handmade goods
Tradeindia	3325	B2B Marketplace
Kompass	4652	B2B Directory
Experian	5606	Credit Report
Globalsources	6025	B2B Marketplace
Diytrade	7560	B2B Trading Platform
Hoovers	8464	Business Database
Hktdc	8705	Global Business Platform
Ecplaza.net	8766	B2B Marketplace
10Times	10738	Business Event Platform
ExportersIndia	11602	B2B Marketplace
Tradekorea	12106	International E-trade Marketplace
Business.com	12580	Marketplace
Shopping	12793	Price Comparison Site
Salespider	13239	Business Social Network
Americanapparel	13857	Fashion Online Shopping
DNB	14292	Credit Report

Thomasnet	15888	Product Sourcing
Ariba	16402	Business Network
Ecrater	20438	Online shopping mall
Taiwantrade.com.tv	20619	Trade Portal
Toocle	22676	B2B Platform
Bizbilla	25286	B2B Marketplace
Ec21	25929	B2B Marketplace
Gobizkorea	26478	International Trade website
Businessseek.biz	26592	Business Directory
Globalmarket	27528	M2B Marketplace
Liquidation	29916	Liquidity services online auction
Lazada.com.my	31923	B2C E-Commerce platform
Efactor	32041	Entrepreneurs Social Network
EventsEye	32403	Trade Show Directory
CeBit.de	33805	Computer Expo
FibretoFashionInt.	39398	B2B Marketplace
Hisupplier	42830	Trade E-Marketplace
Killerstartups	47756	Start-up Community
Crowdcube	55608	Crowdfunding
BuyKorea.org	55752	B2B Marketplace
Go4worldbusiness	56132	B2B Marketplace
ESources.co.uk	58069	Wholesale Directory

Ironplanet	61070	B2B Marketplace
Mercantil	61116	Business Portal
Gulfbusiness.Trade…	62626	B2B Directory
EtradeAsia	66002	E-Marketplace
Infobanc	66007	B2B Trade Portal
Importers	69287	B2B Trade Portal
Leadferret	71753	B2B Database
Indiabizsource	73310	B2B Marketplace
Ecvv	74350	B2B Marketplace
Buyerzone	79542	B2B Marketplace
Importexportplatform	82214	B2B Marketplace
Kmall	85894	Online Shopping Mall
Tradeford	92540	B2B Marketplace
Europages	97854	B2B Website
Tradekey	102482	B2B Marketplace
Tradett	103308	B2B Marketplace
Toptenwholesale	105693	Wholesale Directory
TradeArabia	109882	Business Portal
Businessmagnet.co.uk	110543	B2B Directory
Quataronlinedirectory	114310	Business Directory
Asdonline	117640	Trade Show consumer goods
Rockanddirt	124721	B2B Marketplace
ItalianModa	127063	B2B Marketplace

Tradeboss	131290	B2B Marketplace
Nuorder	137127	Wholesale Marketplace
B2Bindex.co.uk	137385	B2B Directory
BNI	139462	Business Network International
Imexbb	161632	B2B Marketplace
Busytrade	165959	B2B Marketplace
Manufacturer	166043	Manufacturer Directory
Magiconline	173572	B2B Marketplace
Founder2Be	185066	Start-up Community
Zentrada.eu	186155	Wholesale Marketplace
Worldstopexports	195263	Statistics and research
TSNN	196054	Trade Show Directory
Reedexpo	197896	Organizer of exhibitions
B2B.Tradeholding	201579	B2B Directory
BusinessGlobal	201683	Online Exhibitions
ApprovedBusiness	217346	B2B Directory
IndustrySearch.com.au	219717	B2B Marketplace
MFG	231170	Manufacturing Marketplace
Globalbx	236308	Sales of businesses
Achilles	248596	Business Network
Mesteel	267925	B2B Marketplace
Africa-business	268416	Africa Directories
Ewomennetwork	275439	Business Network

Biznik	276570	Entrepreneurial Community
Rusmarket	310406	B2B Portal
Tradeshowalerts	337210	Trade Show Directory
SouthafricaB2B.co.za	347040	B2B Portal
Wholesalepages	353207	Wholesale Suppliers Directory
MyCapital	375427	Venture Capital Network
B2B-directory-uk.co.uk	394130	B2B Directory
Golden-Trade	400276	Business Network
Matchdeck	418650	Business Matching Platform
Toboc	430531	B2B Marketplace
Worldbid	430969	B2B Marketplace
TradeTurkey	440091	B2B Marketplace
Australiatradenow	458419	B2B Marketplace
Industracom	473175	B2B Website
Mercatrade	497259	B2B Portal
Poland-Export	508430	Business Directory
B2Brazil	523196	B2B Trade Portal
Wholesalefashionistas	535064	Wholesale Marketplace
Hospitalityhub	588305	Hospitality B2B Directory
Arbet	596743	Armenian Business Directory
MedicalSearch.com.au	599494	B2B Marketplace
WorldBusinessCulture	605098	Business Culture Information
Insitejapan	616270	B2B Directory

Bestsaexporters	619844	Manufacturer Directory
IraqDirectory	634184	Business Directory
Japaninc	635780	Business Information
TradeEgypt	645547	B2B Marketplace
Bvents	746780	Events Database
Baltic-Leads	759713	Business Portal
Fuzing	783985	B2B Marketplace
NZdirectory.co.nz	832046	Business Directory
Offpriceshow	908202	Wholesale Marketplace fashion
Jordanyp	988454	Business Directory
Brazilbiz.com.br	999285	B2B Marketplace
Angel Investment Network	1081163	Angel Investment Network
CompanyPartners	1252742	Business and Investor Network
Venexport	1534560	B2B Directory
Businesspartners	2122090	Business Network
Wymoo	2510238	Background checks
Centrallia	4015344	B2B Forum
Futurallia	7259817	Organizer of B2B events

SOURCES:

Wikipedia, Alexa, Google, Facebook, LinkedIn, Cambridge Dictionaries Online, E-Commerce Wiki, Investopedia and all websites I mentioned in this book.